T0014685

US AIR FORCE

BY MEG GAERTNER

Apex is distributed by North Star Editions:
sales@northstareditions.com | 888-417-0195

Produced for Apex by Red Line Editorial.

Photographs ©: Shutterstock Images, cover (plane), cover (clouds), 1, 4–5, 6–7, 8–9, 10–11, 12–13, 16–17, 18, 19, 22–23, 24, 25, 26, 29; iStockphoto, 8, 20–21; US Army Signal Corps/AP Images, 14–15

Library of Congress Control Number: 2022901414

ISBN
978-1-63738-310-0 (hardcover)
978-1-63738-346-9 (paperback)
978-1-63738-414-5 (ebook pdf)
978-1-63738-382-7 (hosted ebook)

Printed in the United States of America
Mankato, MN
082022

NOTE TO PARENTS AND EDUCATORS

Apex books are designed to build literacy skills in striving readers. Exciting, high-interest content attracts and holds readers' attention. The text is carefully leveled to allow students to achieve success quickly. Additional features, such as bolded glossary words for difficult terms, help build comprehension.

TABLE OF CONTENTS

CHAPTER 1

BEHIND ENEMY LINES

A C-130 Hercules flies high above enemy land. The back of the plane opens. A pararescue jumper (PJ) dives out.

Pararescue jumpers skydive from airplanes or helicopters.

The PJ free-falls for several thousand feet. Then he opens his **parachute**. He glides down behind enemy lines. A US soldier is being held captive there.

PJs jump from very high up. They wait to open their parachutes until close to the ground.

PJs use night-vision goggles and other gear during their work.

The PJ shoots down two enemy fighters. He finds the hurt US soldier. The PJ quickly provides first aid. Then he brings the soldier to safety.

PJs may land in many types of places. So, they train to run, fight, swim, and climb.

TOUGH TRAINING

PJ training is very challenging. PJs learn many ways to skydive. They train with weapons. They give medical aid. They learn how to survive and avoid enemies.

CHAPTER 2

HIGH-FLYING HISTORY

People have fought by land or sea for centuries. Air combat is much newer. At first, the US Army commanded all air missions.

During World War I (1914–1918), pilots flew small airplanes that were powered by propellers.

Air fights among planes are known as dogfights.

US **pilots** shot at enemy planes. US air power helped end World War II (1939–1945). Pilots dropped two **atomic bombs** on Japan.

In 1947, the US Air Force (USAF) became an **independent** branch of the military. The USAF has protected Americans ever since.

The first group of Black pilots trained in 1941. They were called the Tuskegee Airmen.

BREAKING BARRIERS

At first, Black pilots served in separate units. In 1948, the USAF began work to change that. A few years later, it was the first military branch to become integrated.

CHAPTER 3

MANY MISSIONS

The USAF is divided into several Major Commands. Each one focuses on different jobs. And each is split into several smaller groups. These groups include **wings** and **squadrons**.

Each Major Command uses a different air force base as its headquarters.

Each squadron has a specific purpose. For example, the Thunderbirds squadron flies jet planes.

Some groups focus on fighting or bombing. Some spy and gather information. Others mainly treat wounds.

THUNDERBIRDS

The Thunderbirds perform air shows around the world. The pilots fly close together. They make shapes and patterns. And they show off their skill. Many people come to watch them.

Thunderbirds perform in an airshow at Nellis Air Force Base in Nevada in 2010.

The USAF doesn't just fight. Pilots also spray water to stop wildfires. They fly into hurricanes to study them. They bring food, water, and supplies to areas in need.

FAST FACT

In December 2021, the USAF had about 320,000 active members.

PJs rescue people after natural disasters such as hurricanes. They use helicopters to save people from flooded areas.

CHAPTER 4

CALLED TO SERVE

S ome people join the USAF as enlisted airmen. Others become officers. Officers lead other airmen.

Members of the USAF wear uniforms. These clothes may vary depending on their rank or task.

Fighter pilots train to fly fast jets, such as the F-16 Fighting Falcon.

All USAF members train for months. They learn how to fight and use weapons. They learn to stay calm during combat. Then members learn their specific jobs.

Training helps USAF members practice their skills, such as parachuting from planes.

SPACE FORCE

The US Space Force formed in 2019. It is a new military branch. Members maintain satellites. These objects circle Earth. They collect and send important information. Members also launch rockets, develop new technology, and more.

The USAF has more than 200 job options. Some people design or repair airplanes. Others fly them. All members work toward protecting American lives.

◀ Workers load weapons onto a B-52 bomber at Barksdale Air Force Base.

COMPREHENSION QUESTIONS

Write your answers on a separate piece of paper.

1. Write a sentence that explains the main ideas of Chapter 3.

2. Which type of job in the USAF would you be most interested in having? Why?

3. When did the USAF become an independent branch of the military?

    A. in the mid-1800s

    B. in 1947

    C. in 2019

4. Why does training for pararescue jumpers include learning to use weapons?

    A. All PJ missions involve only fighting.

    B. A PJ mission may involve stealing weapons.

    C. A PJ may need to get past enemies during a mission.

5. What does **combat** mean in this book?

People have fought by land or sea for centuries. Air combat is much newer.

    A. sailing
    B. fighting
    C. flying

6. What does **options** mean in this book?

The USAF has more than 200 job options. Some people design or repair airplanes. Others fly them.

    A. things people can choose
    B. things people can't see
    C. things people don't know

Answer key on page 32.

GLOSSARY

ace
A pilot who has shot down at least five enemy aircraft.

atomic bombs
Powerful weapons that can wipe out entire cities.

independent
Able to make decisions without being controlled by another group.

integrated
No longer dividing people into groups based on race.

parachute
Fabric that opens up to slow a person's fall through the air.

pilots
People who fly aircraft.

squadrons
Relatively small groups of soldiers and vehicles that are sent out to do certain tasks.

wings
Relatively large groups of soldiers made up of several squadrons.

TO LEARN MORE

BOOKS

Abdo, Kenny. *United States Air Force*. Minneapolis: Abdo Publishing, 2019.

Murray, Julie. *US Space Force*. Minneapolis: Abdo Publishing, 2021.

Ringstad, Arnold. *US Air Force Equipment and Vehicles*. Minneapolis: Abdo Publishing, 2022.

ONLINE RESOURCES

Visit **www.apexeditions.com** to find links and resources related to this title.

ABOUT THE AUTHOR

Meg Gaertner is a children's book editor and writer who lives in Minnesota. Her grandfather flew a P-47 Thunderbolt in World War II.

INDEX

ANSWER KEY:
1. Answers will vary; 2. Answers will vary; 3. B; 4. C; 5. B; 6. A